You've Done It Again, Charlie Brown

Selected Cartoons from WE'RE RIGHT BEHIND
YOU, CHARLIE BROWN Volume II

Charles M. Schulz

CORONET BOOKS
Hodder Fawcett, London

Copyright © 1958, 1959, 1960, 1961, 1962, 1963, 1964
by United Feature Syndicate Inc.

First Published by Fawcett Publications Inc.,
New York

Coronet edition 1971
Eighth impression 1978

Printed in Great Britain for Hodder
Fawcett Ltd., Mill Road, Dunton Green,
Sevenoaks, Kent. (Editorial Office:
47 Bedford Square, London, WC1 3DP) by
C. Nicholls & Company Ltd.,
The Philips Park Press, Manchester

ISBN 0 340 12521 7

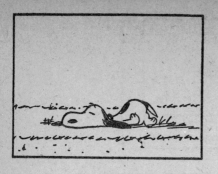

I IMAGINE THAT EVEN AN INEXPENSIVE FIELDER'S GLOVE WOULD LAST A PLAYER LIKE HIM FOR YEARS!

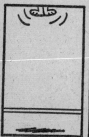

THE EARLY MORNING LIGHT REVEALS A VULTURE PERCHED HIGH ON THE LIMB OF A TREE

AH! A VICTIM!

I SUPPOSE IF I TOLD YOU THERE'S A VULTURE OUTSIDE THAT'S BOTHERING ME YOU'D SAY I WAS CRAZY, WOULDN'T YOU?

YES, I WOULD!

ONE FINGER WILL MEAN A FAST BALL, TWO
FINGERS A CURVE AND THREE FINGERS
A SLOW BALL...OKAY?

FINE

EMPTY! AND I'M
DYING OF THIRST!

THAT'S ONE I'M GOING TO HAVE TO THINK ABOUT FOR AWHILE!

ZIP!

THUS ENDETH THE DIVING CAREER!

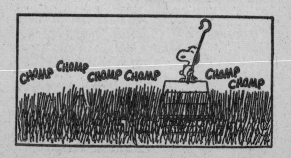

WHERE WERE YOU FEBRUARY 14th WHEN EVERYONE ELSE WAS GIVING OUT VALENTINES? IS KINDNESS AND THOUGHTFULNESS SOMETHING YOU CAN MAKE RETROACTIVE? DON'T YOU THINK HE HAS ANY FEELINGS?!

YOU AND YOUR FRIENDS ARE THE MOST THOUGHTLESS BUNCH I'VE EVER KNOWN! YOU DON'T CARE ANYTHING ABOUT CHARLIE BROWN! YOU JUST HATE TO FEEL GUILTY!

AND NOW YOU HAVE THE NERVE TO COME AROUND A WHOLE MONTH LATER, AND OFFER HIM A USED VALENTINE JUST TO EASE YOUR CONSCIENCE! WELL, LET ME TELL YOU SOMETHING... CHARLIE BROWN DOESN'T NEED YOUR...

DON'T INTERFERE...I'LL TAKE IT!

AND I FEEL THAT AS LONG AS WE HAVE TO LIVE TOGETHER IN THE SAME FAMILY, WE SHOULD TRY TO GET ALONG...

I JUST THINK WE COULD WORK A LITTLE HARDER AT IT, THAT'S ALL...DO YOU AGREE?

YOU'RE RIGHT...TALKING TO LUCY IS LIKE TALKING TO A BRICK WALL!